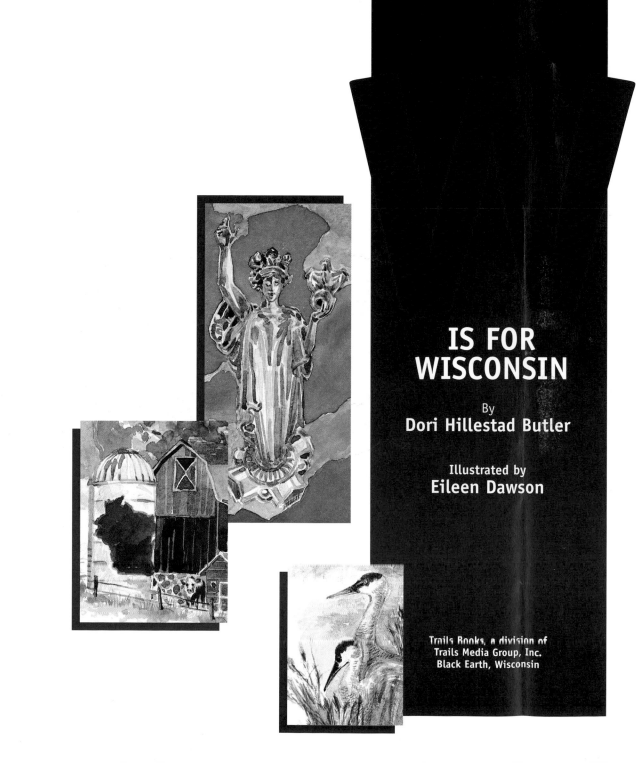

IS FOR WISCONSIN

By
Dori Hillestad Butler

Illustrated by
Eileen Dawson

Trails Books, a division of
Trails Media Group, Inc.
Black Earth, Wisconsin

In memory of my grandparents, Martin and Edna Dietrich.
D.H.B.

For David A. Spitzer, whose creative, considerate and comprehensive approach to teaching inspired and illuminated these illustrations.
E.D.

A

is for Apostle Islands.

The Apostle Islands are Wisconsin's northernmost point. According to Ojibwe legend, the islands were formed when the god Winneboujou tracked a deer from his home on the Brule River to the shores of Lake Superior. He tried to shoot the deer with his arrows, but the deer escaped into the lake. Frustrated, Winneboujou threw a handful of rocks at the deer, and the rocks became islands. When French explorers arrived in Wisconsin, they counted 12 islands and named them for the 12 Apostles of Jesus. There are actually 22 islands.

Adel · Albany · Alma · Albion · Allouez · Alverno · Amberg · Amery · Amherst · Aniwa · Antigo · Apple Creek

Appleton · Arbor Vitae · Argyle · Arkdale · Arlington

Armstrong Creek · Arnott

Athelstane · Ashwaubenon · Athens · Atlas · Attica · Auburndale · Avoca · Aztalan · Auroraville · Avon

Arthur · Ashland   Ashippun ·   Ashton Corners

a

B

is for Badger.

Wisconsin's nickname is the "Badger State." During the 1820s, Cornish miners dug burrows into the hillsides around Mineral Point, hoping to strike lead. Some miners even lived in these burrows. The holes were just like those dug by furry badgers, so people called the miners "badgers." Eventually the nickname came to refer to all Wisconsinites. Today, "Bucky Badger" is the University of Wisconsin's mascot.

b

Babcock • Bagley • Baileys Harbor • Bakerville • Balsam Lake • Bangor • Baraboo • Barneveld • Barron • Basco

Belleville • Belmont • Beloit • Birchwood • Black Earth • Black River Falls

Bay City • Bayfield • Bear Creek • Beaver Dam • Beetown • Belgium • Berlin

THE VOTE f ★ r WOMEN

Crivitz · Cross Plains · Cuba City

YES VOTE FOR

VOTE ★ WOMEN

Columbus · Coon Valley · Cornucopia

Cable · Cadott · Cambridge · Camp Douglas · Cashton · Cassville

VOTES YES WOMEN

Cataract · Cazenovia · Cedarburg · Chetek · Chilton · Chippewa Falls · Clam Lake · Clear Lake · Clyde · Colby · Colfax

C
is for
Carrie Chapman Catt.

Carrie Chapman Catt was born in Ripon in 1859. She was 13 years old when she discovered that women couldn't vote in elections. She didn't think that was fair, so when she grew up, she joined the suffrage movement. The people in the suffrage movement pressured the government to give women the right to vote. Catt became one of their most important leaders. Congress granted women the right to vote on Aug. 18, 1920, when it passed the 19th Amendment to the Constitution. Wisconsin was the first state to ratify the amendment.

D

is for Dairy.

Wisconsin is known as America's Dairyland. The state's 1.4 million cows produce more than 2.7 billion gallons of milk every year. Nearly 88 percent of that milk is made into cheese. It takes 10 pounds of milk to make just one pound of cheese. Wisconsin manufactures more cheese than any other state. Cheesemakers here make 300 different varieties, types and styles of cheese, including Colby, Swiss, cheddar, brick and Limburger. Colby and brick cheese were invented in Wisconsin. Limburger cheese is made only in Wisconsin and in Europe.

Dairy Center · Dairyland · Dakota · Daleyville · Danbury · Danville · Dane · Darien · Darlington · De Pere · De Soto

Dilly · Dodgeville · Donald · Dorchester · Dousman · Draper · Dresser · Drummond · Duck Creek · Dundee

Deer Park · Deerbrook

Deerfield · Dekorra · Deforest · Delafield

d

Delavan · Dell · Denmark · Denzer · Devils Corner · Dexter · Dheinsville · Diamond Grove · Dickeyville

E

is for Earth Day.

During the 1960s, Wisconsin Senator Gaylord Nelson wanted people to understand that we needed to take better care of the planet. He designated April 22, 1970, as the first "Earth Day." More than 20 million people nationwide listened to speeches, participated in demonstrations and took action to clean up the environment on that day. Today, Earth Day is an international event that involves more than 200 million people from 140 countries.

Eagle · Eagle River · Earl · Eastman · Eau Claire · Eau Galle · Ebenezer

Egg Harbor · Eleva · Elk Grove · Elkhart Lake · Elkhorn · Ellison Bay · Elroy

Eden · Edgerton · Edgewater · Eureka

F

is for French Fur Trade.

The first white men to visit present-day Wisconsin were French fur traders. During the 17th and 18th centuries, they set up trading posts in Green Bay and Prairie du Chien and on the Apostle Islands. They gave the Native Americans mirrors, knives, guns and trinkets in exchange for beaver fur. The fur trade led to European settlement of the Midwest.

Fairfield · Fair Play

Fall Creek · Fall River · Fargo · Farmers Valley · Fern

Farmington · Fayette · Fennimore · Ferryville

Footville · Forest Junction · Fort Atkinson · Fort McCoy · Fountain City · Four Corners · Forward

Fifield · Fish Creek · Fitchburg · Fitzgerald · Five Corners · Flintville · Florence · Folsom · Fond du Lac · Fontana

f

g

Gad · Galesville · Galloway · Garfield · Gays Mills · Genesee Depot · Genoa · Germania · Germantown · Gibbsville

Green Lake

Gilbert · Gills Rock · Gilmanton · Gleason · Glen Flora · Glencoe · Gurney

Glendale · Glidden · Gooseville · Gotham

WORLD PROFESSIONAL FOOTBALL CHAMPIONSHIP

Grafton · Grand Marsh · Grantsburg · Gratiot

G

is for
Green Bay Packers.

The Green Bay Packers are the only publicly owned football team in the nation. The club began in 1919 when a Green Bay meat-packing company put up money for equipment. When the packing company backed out, Green Bay businesses bought stock for $5 a share. The Packers were the first team to have cheerleaders, the first to have a public-address system and the first to have a mascot—a dog named Olive. They have won more world championships than any other team in the National Football League.

H
is for
Harry Houdini.

Harry Houdini (whose real name was Erich Weiss) was born in Budapest, Hungary, in 1874, but he grew up in Appleton. He was one of the most famous magicians in American history. He could escape from jails, straight-jackets, milk cans, sealed coffins and his famous Chinese Water Torture Cell. The Chinese Water Torture Cell was a large glass tank. The tank was filled with water, and Houdini was lowered into it upside down. His feet were chained to the top. He could escape in minutes. Houdini could also walk through a brick wall, stop a pulse and make a 10,000-pound elephant disappear on stage.

Hamburg · Hancock · Hales Corners · Hannibal · Hanover · Harmony · Harrison · Holt

Hub City · Hortonville · Horicon · Honey Creek · Hólmen · Hollister · Hollandale

Harshaw · Hartford · Hartland · Hatfield · Haugen · Haven · Hayward · Hazel Green · Hazelhurst · Hebron

Heffron · Helena · Herbster · Highcliff · Hilbert · Hildas Corner · Hillsboro · Hillside · Hixton · Holcombe

Imalone • Independence • Indian Creek • Indianford • Ingersoll • Ingram • Inlet • Ino • Institute • Ipswich

Iron Belt • Iron Ridge • Iron River • Ironton • Irving • Irvington • Itasca • Ithaca

I

is for Ice Age.

About 30,000 years ago, a huge mass of ice crept down from the Canadian highlands. It covered two-thirds of present-day Wisconsin and is known as the Wisconsin glacier. The glacier smashed, scraped or buried almost everything in its path. Its grinding movement, along with the water that rushed from it as it melted, created thousands of lakes and rivers, gently rolling hills and exotic rock formations like the Wisconsin Dells. Wisconsin's Ice Age Trail is a National Scenic Trail that generally follows the southern edge of the glacier's path. When the trail is completed, it will be a thousand miles long.

J

is for Jump Rope.

Bloomer is known as the "Speed Rope-Jumping Capital of the World." On the last Saturday in January, the Bloomer school district hosts a speed rope-jumping contest. People come from all over Wisconsin to show how many jumps they can make in 10 seconds. On January 27, 1979, Paul Morning set a world's record for speed rope-jumping. He jumped 74 times in 10 seconds.

Jackson · Jacksonport · Jacksonville · Jamestown   Janesville · Jefferson · Jefferson Junction

Johnsonville · Johnston · Johnston Center · Jonesdale · Jordan

Jenkynsville

Jennings · Jericho · Jersey City · Jewett

Johnsburg · Johnson Creek

Jim Falls   Jimtown · Joel · Johannesburg · Juda

ROPE JUMP CONTEST
J
BLOOMER, WI

K

is for Kleenex® Tissue.

In 1924, the Kimberly & Clark Company in Neenah introduced Kleenex Kerchiefs, the world's first facial tissue. Hollywood and Broadway stars used Kleenex Kerchiefs to wipe off stage makeup, so Kimberly & Clark advertised them as a scientific and glamorous way for sophisticated women to remove makeup and cold cream. The company was shocked to discover people were using the kerchiefs to blow their noses! A package of 100 6-inch by 7-inch sheets originally sold for 65 cents.

Kalinke · Kansasville · Kaukauna · Keene · Kegonsa · Kekoskee · Kellner · Kelly · Kendall · Kennan · Kennedy · Kiel

Kenosha · Keshena · Kewaskum · Kewaunee · Keyeser · Kickapoo Center · Kilbournville · Krok

Kimberly · King · Kingston · Kirby · Klevenville · Klondike · Knapp · Kohler · Koro · Koshkonong · Krakow

L

is for Lumberjack.

Until the 1850s, huge pine trees grew in northern Wisconsin. Then lumberjacks cut down almost all of the forest. During the winter, a lumberjack worked from sunrise to sunset, chopping trees that were sometimes 400 years old and up to 10 feet in diameter. A two-man team could chop a hundred pine logs in one day. When spring came, lumberjacks tumbled the logs into the rushing rivers and herded them downstream to the sawmills. The wood was used to build houses in the big cities. Wisconsin is still a leading lumber state, but lumber companies now plant more trees than they cut down.

La Crosse · La Farge · La Grange · La Pointe

Lehigh · Lemonweir · Lena · Levis · Liberty Pole · Lily · Lime Ridge

La Rue · Lac du Flambeau · Ladoga · Ladysmith · Lake Delton · Lake Como · Lake Geneva · Lake Mills

Lake Wissota · Lakewood   Lamar · Lancaster · Land O' Lakes · Langlade · Laona · Lebanon · Leeds

m

Maiden Rock · Manawa · Manitowish Waters · Manitowoc · Marengo · Maribel · Marshfield · Mineral Point

Mercer · Merrill · Merrimac · Millston · Milwaukee · Milton

Mauston · Mayville · Mazomanie · Mecan · Medford · Mellen

Menasha · Menomonee Falls · Menomonie · Mequon

M

is for Madison.

Wisconsin became a territory in 1836. Lawmakers met in Belmont that first year. One of the first things they had to do was decide on a permanent location for the capital city. Politician James Doty suggested an empty woodland between two beautiful lakes, halfway between Lake Michigan and the Mississippi River. The city was named "Madison" in honor of President James Madison, who died that summer. Today, the state capitol building sits on Madison's highest hill. It was built in 1917 as a smaller replica of the nation's capitol building in Washington, D.C. Its dome is the only granite dome in the country.

N

**is for
Native American.**

People first came to
Wisconsin about 12,000
years ago, when the Ice Age
was ending. Since then,
Wisconsin has been home
to many Native American
cultures, including the Old
Copper Culture, the first
people in the Americas to
create metal; the Mound
Builders, who built huge
animal-shaped earthen
mounds; and the Hopewell,
who were highly skilled
farmers, traders and artists.
When white settlers arrived
in the 1800s, the main
Native American tribes were
the Ojibwe, Menominee,
Ho-Chunk, Sioux, Ottawa and
Potawatomi. Today, about
40,000 Native Americans live
in the state.

Nabob · Namekagon · Nashotah · Navarino · Necedah · Neillsville · Nekoosa · Nelson · Neopit · Neshkoro · Nora

Norske

Northport · Norwalk · Norway Grove

New Berlin · New Glarus · New London · Niagara

Northland

n

Oak Grove · Oconomowoc

Osseo · Otsego

Oconto · Odanah · Ogema

Ukauchee · Unalaska

O

is for Old Abe.

During the Civil War, the soldiers of the Eighth Wisconsin regiment of Eau Claire bought a bald eagle for $5 and named him "Old Abe," after President Abraham Lincoln. He became their mascot. When the troops marched, Old Abe carried a corner of the American flag in his beak. During battles, he flew over Southern troops and screeched at them. The South even offered a reward to any soldier who could shoot him. After the war, Old Abe lived in the basement of the capitol building. When a fire broke out in the building, the eagle breathed in too much smoke. He died a few weeks later on March 26, 1881.

P

is for Peshtigo Fire.

The summer of 1871 was unusually hot and dry in northeastern Wisconsin. During the late summer and early fall, forest fires sprang up. On October 8, 1871, one of these fires roared through the forest, fueled by strong winds and drying branches left on the ground by the logging companies. The fire killed 1,200 people, and destroyed the entire town of Peshtigo and more than a million acres of forestland. The Peshtigo fire was among the nation's deadliest fires, yet no national newspaper covered the story. That's because on the same night, a major fire broke out in Chicago. That fire killed 200 people.

Portage · Port Washington

Pigeon Corners · Poniatowski · Plymouth · Plover

Packwaukee · Palmyra · Paoli · Pardeeville · Park Falls · Parnell · Patch Grove · Pembine

Pence · Pepin · Perkinstown · Pewaukee · Phelps · Phillips · Pigeon Falls

p

Quarry · Queenstown · Quinney · Quarry · Queenstown · Quinney · Quarry · Queenstown · Quinney · Queenstown

q

Q

is for Quarry.

During the late 1800s and early 1900s, the Montello Granite Quarry was known throughout the United States. Judges at the 1893 World's Fair declared red Montello granite "100 percent harder than any other granite." Builders used it for President Ulysses S. Grant's tomb in New York City and for many buildings in the Midwest. It also was used for gravestones and roads.

R

is for
Ringling Brothers.

The Ringling family circus was one of more than a hundred circuses that got its start in Wisconsin. It was founded in 1884. The circus traveled around the country during the summer and spent winters in Baraboo, sewing costumes and training elephants, horses and tigers. In the early 1900s, the Ringling Brothers bought out their largest competitor, Barnum and Bailey, and declared their new circus the "Greatest Show on Earth."

Racine · Readstown · Redgranite   Reedsburg · Retreat · Rio · Rusk

ALF. T.

Romance · Rome

Ringling BROS

World's Greatest Shows

CIRCUS

Rhinelander

AL

Rib Falls · Rib Lake · Rice Lake

Richland Center

JOHN

CHARLES

OTTO

S

is for Spaniel.

The American water spaniel is Wisconsin's state dog. The breed was developed in the 1920s by Dr. Fred Pfeifer of New London. These short, brown, curly-haired, sharp-eyed dogs are bred for hunting, but their intelligence, loyalty and comradeship make them nice companions for children, as well. The American water spaniel is the only breed that was developed in Wisconsin, and it is one of only five breeds developed in the United States.

Sandusky · Sarona · Sauk City · Saukville · Saxeville · Saxon · Sayner · Schofield · Seeley · Seymour · Shawano

Stevens Point

Sharon · Sheboygan · Shell Lake

Shiocton · Shorewood · Shullsburg · Sinsinawa · Siren · Sister Bay

T

is for Trilobite.

The trilobite (pronounced TRY-loh-bite) is Wisconsin's state fossil. Trilobites were flat shellfish that crawled along the bottom of the warm, shallow, salty sea that covered Wisconsin during the Paleozoic Era. They were among the first animals to have eyes. The name trilobite means "three-lobed." A trilobite's shell was in three sections. As the animal grew, it shed its shell and grew a new one. Many trilobite fossils are actually fossils of the discarded shell rather than of the animal itself. At one time, there were thousands of trilobite species around the world, but they all died out 240 million years ago.

Tabor · Tadpole Corners · Tamarack · Taycheedah · Taylor · Tell · Tennyson · Theresa · Thiensville · Thompson

Turtle Lake · Tuscobia · Twelve Corners

Eye

Thornapple · Thorp · Three Lakes · Tiffany · Tigerton

Tilden · Timberland · Token Creek

Trego · Tripoli · Troy · Tunnelville

Tipler · Tomah · Tomahawk · Townsend · Trempealeau

And by virtue of the power, and for the purpose aforesaid, I do order and declare that all persons held as slaves within said designated States; and parts of States are, and henceforth shall be free; and that

Abraham Lincoln.

Utley • Utowana Beach

Ubet • Ulao • Underhill • Union Center

Un on Grove • Unity • Upson • Urne • Utica

Union Church

U

is for
Underground Railroad.

The Underground Railroad was a network of people who provided shelter to runaway slaves in the mid-19th century. The Milton House, which was a hotel operated by the Goodrich family in Janesville, was one "stop" on the railroad. Runaway slaves entered the Goodrich cabin, opened a trap door in the cabin floor and followed a tunnel from the cabin to the basement of the Milton House. There, the family gave them food and shelter and helped them get to the next stop on their journey to freedom in Canada.

u

V

is for Vitamins.

In 1907, Dr. Elmer V. McCollum, professor of agricultural chemistry at the University of Wisconsin, discovered that if rats ate only grains, they eventually became blind. But if green leafy vegetables, butter or cod liver oil was added to their diets, their sight returned. This led to the discovery of Vitamin A. McCollum helped discover several other vitamins. He also came up with the "letter system" of naming vitamins.

Valders · Valley · Valley Junction · Veefkind · Valton · Van Buskirk · Van Dyne · Vandreuil · Veedum · Valmy

Van Buskirk · Van Dyne · Vandreuil · Veedum

Vernon

Vinnie Ha Ha · Vesper

Vernon Station · Verona

Victory · Victory Center · Victory Heights · Vienna · Vignes · Viking · Vilas · Viola · Virocqua · Victory Center

W

is for Wisconsin.

Wisconsin is a beautiful Midwestern state with large forests, small farmsteads, gentle hills, winding rivers and 15,000 lakes. It was named for the Wisconsin River, which flows through the central part of the state and empties into the Mississippi River. Native Americans called the river the "Meskousing," which means "where the waters gather." The French spelled the word "Ouisconsin." The English used a variety of spellings before settling on the one that we use today. Wisconsin became the nation's 30th state on May 29, 1848.

Wabeno · Wagner · Wales   Walworth · Warrens · Washburn · Waterloo · Watertown

Whitefish Bay

Waukesha · Waunakee · Waupaca · Waupun · Wausau

Webster · West Allis · West Bend · Westby   Wyocena   Wyalusing

X

**is for
X-Country Skiing.**

When Scandinavian
immigrants came to
Wisconsin, they brought
x-country skis with them.
They used the skis to glide
on top of the deep snow.
Today, many people enjoy
x-country skiing in
Wisconsin. The Birkebeiner,
North America's largest
x-country ski race, is held
every February between
Cable and Hayward. More
than 6,000 people from
around the world participate
in the race each year.

Y

**is for
Yerkes Observatory.**

Located on the shores of
Lake Geneva, Yerkes
Observatory is a research
facility that is operated by
the University of Chicago.
It was completed in 1897.
It houses a 40-inch refractor
telescope, the largest
telescope of its kind ever
built. One of the things
scientists use it for is to
study the movement of stars.
Photos taken today can be
compared with photos taken
a hundred years ago with
the same instrument.

Yarnell · Yellow Lake · Yellowstone ·   York · Yorkville

Z

**is for
Milwaukee County Zoo.**

The Milwaukee County Zoo began as a small mammal and bird display in 1882. It was one of the first zoos in the country to do away with small cages and allow animals to roam in more natural settings. Today, it is home to approximately 2,500 animals—300 different species of mammals, reptiles, birds, fish and invertebrates.

Zachow

Zander · Zenda